A Wife Prays

By ROY G. GESCH

Concordia Publishing House

St. Louis

Concordia Publishing House, St. Louis, Missouri

© 1968 Concordia Publishing House
Library of Congress Catalog Card No. 68-22575

Second Printing 1970

Manufactured in the United States of America

To Dorothy

*who has shown me how wonderful
a good marriage can be*

Contents

Preface

To you newlyweds, congratulations!
To you not so newly wed —
isn't marriage wonderful?

God has brought you two together. Now it is my prayer that you two may be as one in all your years ahead. With that in mind, this book is offered to you in the hope that it may help to deepen and enrich that oneness.

The first section reminds you of what you have promised to each other and to God when you made your marriage vows. It lets you talk over with God what marriage is intended to be.

The second section is made up of some of the common complaints, the usual trouble spots, that can have a definite effect on marriage — that can either strengthen or weaken the oneness and happiness of it. Since husband and wife do not always see a problem in the same way, a double approach is used, in the hope that it will lead to a discussion of the problem. A deeper appreciation of each other's feelings may be as important as an actual solution. The two companion volumes with identical tables of contents permit individual use, whether you are at home together or separated for a few days.

The topics included have not been drawn blindly. In 20 years of marital counseling, a few things have become apparent. One's own personality traits and attitudes are far more damaging to a marriage than external.pressures. There would be fewer divorces, less unhappiness in marriage, less shallowness, if both husband and wife would face up to those potential trouble areas. They may seem trivial and insignificant, but if allowed to grow and become deeply engrained in the fiber of the marriage, they can eventually become great enough to destroy the marriage.

May God bless your marriage!
May He give you a little taste of heaven in it!

ROY G. GESCH

Whittier, California

1
The Essence of Marriage

I Thee Wed

"I take thee to be my wedded husband."

Dear Father above, I smile now
    when I recall the momentary misgivings
        that preceded those words of promise.
You know how much I loved him, Lord,
    and anxiously awaited
        and prepared for that day.
But I got so caught up
    in the whirlwind of activity
        of showers and arrangements,
           in the partying that precedes,
    that I almost forgot
        what it was really all about.
Suddenly certain thoughts began to flash:
    "for all the rest of my life" —
        "with this one particular man" —
"for better or for worse, for richer or for
poorer,
        in sickness or in health."
It all seemed so stunningly final.

But now again I am so grateful, Father,
    that You planned our course of life
        so that our paths not only crossed
           but merged.

Thank you for my husband.
   Life has become so much fuller, deeper,
   and richer
   because of him.

Help me, Lord, to make and keep my marriage
   something beautiful and sacred,
      as You intended it to be.
Let me never lose my joyous wonder,
   as our lives become more fully invested
      in each other's;
   as we live, not only with
      but for each other;
   as our sense of being one
      pervades our every move.

Keep me mindful too, dearest Father,
   that these joys and blessings are mine
      because of You.
Nor let me forget
   that this blessed tie that binds
      is not unlike the bond of love
   that has united me with You.
It all begins with Your love, Father.
   Thank You, Father, for that love.

Hi-Fidelity Promise

"I pledge my faithfulness in every duty."

Lord Jesus, I remember
    that part of the wedding promise
        centered on the question
    "Wilt thou keep thee only unto him?"
I answered unhesitatingly,
    "I will."
It was more than a statement of intent.
    I considered it and still do regard it
        a sacred vow
            that I will keep inviolate.

A sacred vow —
    not just a legal contract
        or a civil agreement.
A sacred vow —
    spoken from the heart to the heart —
        upon which we implored Your blessing.
Lord, keep me faithful to my vow
    and to my beloved husband.

Help me to see that the heart of the promise,
    and certainly of the marriage itself,
        is love —
    love that is recognizable
        in my every thought and attitude,

love that is clearly evident
in everything I do or say —
not just in those moments
of sublime togetherness
but also when we are alone and apart,
as we are so much of so many days.

Give me the kind of love
that makes "faithfulness in every duty"
possible.
Without it marriage is an empty, lifeless shell,
affording a measure of retreat
from some of the world's hard knocks
but little else.

Keep me faithful, as You are faithful, dear Lord.
My promise in my marriage is small
compared with all the promises You
made
to us and for us.
If I find myself questioning the cost
of keeping my word and marriage intact,
let me think of You
and the price You paid
that we might be eternally with You.
You took upon Yourself
the callouses and heartbreaks
of a sick and sinful world,
even the pain and shame
of a sacrificial death;

for such was Your promise,
and such is Your love.

Make me more like You, Lord,
faithful and true in every way.

Till Death Us Do Part

"Till death us do part."

Dear Father, how often I sit
and think about this strange
and wonderful bond called marriage.

There are so many other personal relationships —
in clubs and interest groups,
business partnerships,
friends, and social contacts.
In every one of them,
at some time or other,
I'm looking for a way out.
I become irritated and tired of them.
I am so thankful they are not intended
as a permanent arrangement.

Yet as grateful as I am for their impermanence,
so grateful am I conversely
that marriage is meant to last.

17

It was in deep sincerity
    that I made my lifelong promise
        to the much-loved man of my choosing.
It is in great determined joy
    that I ask You to help me keep my vow
        holy and unbroken until death.
It means so much to think of sharing
    and growing in a love
        that does more than blossom a few
        hours
            in the morning of our lives.
As You planned and willed it to be, Father,
    ours is a love that matures,
        that becomes deeper and richer
            with the passage of time.

I can envision it to be almost a taste
    of Your love for us —
        a love that didn't lessen
            in the centuries of human folly;
        that finally offered, in its fullness,
        the way to life and peace in Christ;
        a love that is as unchangeable
            and eternal as You are.

It's strange, isn't it, Father,
    that when one rests secure in unending
    love,
        words and patterns change?
Even words like "death" and "part,"
    in the promise we made,
        lose their somber note.

All I can think of is
that we are together for all of life.

Male and Female

Dearest Father, I remember
when I announced I was getting married,
there were those who were much
concerned
as to whether I knew the facts of life.
I appreciate their concern,
for I realize many marriages are hurt
by attitudes that reflect
an unfortunate and inadequate
understanding of sex.

It's apparent to me now that,
of all the things I was told to remember,
what Your Word says is the most
important:
"Male and female created He them. . . ."
"A man shall cleave to his wife,
and they shall be one flesh. . . ."
"God saw everything He had made,
and behold, it was very good."

Sometimes it is hard to retain
the feeling that it is good, Father,

19

when you sense that so many about you
        do not know the difference
between affection and lust,
        and couldn't care less.
I pray You, Father,
    that our moments of marital closeness
        may ever be
    not just diversions
        of adventure and play
    but true expressions of deepest love.

And may we be so fully one
    that we can also speak intimately
    to each other of needs and desires,
    as well as barriers and hindrances
        to their fulfillment.
For I know all too well, Father,
    how ice walls can build up
        between two people who cannot share
        their inner thoughts and feelings,
    even though they really do care for each
    other.

Father, may our moments of oneness
    ever be moments of true happiness
        and appreciation
            of what You made to be so good.

Leave and Cleave!

Sometimes I wonder, Lord, why You said:
    "A man leaves his father and his mother
        and cleaves to his wife."
It seems You should have said:
    "A woman leaves her father and her
    mother
        and cleaves to her husband."
Isn't it usually the girl
    who goes home to mother?

You've seen that in me too,
    haven't You, Lord?
You know how much I love my husband
    and cherish our life together.
Yet there were times when I too
    was prone to run to my parents
        to bolster my side in a disagreement.
After all, how could he win
    when the deck was stacked against him,
        with his mother-in-law as trump card?

But I realize that in married life
    there must be a growing up,
        a maturing process,
    on my part as well as his.
Part of our oneness must always be
    facing our problems together —
        our differences of opinion, too.

Good marriages are not the result
　　of people running away from each other
　　　　or hiding from each other
　　or looking for others
　　　　on whom to push their burdens.

Lord, I'm asking You to help me
　　live up to my responsibilities
in furthering and deepening our oneness —
　　our oneness with You too.
I know that Jesus redeemed me from all
　　that might separate me from You.
Make me, for whom that price was paid,
　　be willing to leave all
　　　　that might once again estrange me
　　and prevent me from receiving
　　　　all Your love and grace provides.

Help me catch the secret
　　of such cleaving,
　　　　of such oneness,
　　for both my spiritual life
　　　　and my family life.

That Life May Go On

Dearest Lord Jesus, how very, very right,
　　how completely expressive
　　　　of God's ways of love,

22

is the whole process of generating life,
   the miracle of conceiving
      and giving birth to a child.

How very, very right
   and completely expressive
      of God's ways of love
   was Your way of coming into this world
      to be our Lord and Savior.
"When the fullness of the time was come,
   God sent forth His Son,
      made of a woman."

And so for You also, Lord Jesus,
   earthly life began
      close to the heart of Your mother,
   whose love and whose prayers
      were lavished upon You
   long before she could wrap You
      in swaddling clothes
         and lay You in a manger.

How beautifully You have honored
   and sanctified the process of birth
      by entering our life and world
         as You did.
I believe that I treasure it all the more
   just because of the Christmas story.

"Be fruitful and multiply,"
   our Creator-Father said at the beginning,
      as He blessed us with the ability
   to continue His work of creating new life.

I am truly thankful for this blessing
and for the prospect of having children
and raising a family.

Lord, it may not be my lot
to experience this blessing personally.
(It has been so with many another.)
Should this be true with me,
let me bow to Your better judgment,
confident that Your love
will compensate in other ways.

Should the privilege of conceiving life
and bearing a child be mine,
let me show my joy and gratitude
in prayers of thanks to You
and in the way I lovingly care for
the child whom You would make my
own.

The Role of a Husband

All-discerning Father, spare me the womanly
inclination
to sit, arms akimbo,
in toe-tapping silence,
as if to say:

"Well, I've read what the Bible says
about the duties of husbands!
When are you going to start
living up to it?"

Open my eyes to an awareness
that when one gives,
there's more to it
than that the other just take and take.
Make me appreciative
and, to a degree at least, worthy
of my husband's self-giving love.

Dispel from my mind the popular fallacy
that marriage is a 50-50 proposition.
You've asked that the husband
give himself up for his wife,
as Christ gave Himself up for us all.
That's 100 percent! Completely! All!
Now help me to see
that when one gives completely in love,
the only proper response is
that the recipient in turn
give completely in love.
Even logically it makes sense!
A 200% investment is bound to be better
than one of 100%.
A marriage in which two in love
give themselves completely to each
other
stands double the chance
of true joy and blessing.

Bless our home with such all-giving love,
Father,
    his for me
        and mine for him.

And Father, if days should come
    when we begin to think too much of
    ourselves,
        and too little of each other,
refocus our attention on Jesus
    and what love really is.
Forgive us our moments of lovelessness.
    Help us to enter each day
        so filled with unselfish love
            that we may truly live
        for each other
            and for You.

The Role of a Wife

Holy Father, I want to be a good wife.
I want to live up to everything You've said
    a perfect wife should be.

Some things I can easily grasp —
    statements like "let the wife see
        that she respects her husband."

But I stumble at times
on words like "subject" and "submit"
when You use them in describing
the wife's relationship to her husband.

I suppose it's because we immediately
conjure up visions
of "Yes, master! No, master!"
of female inferiority,
and of being used like a doormat.
But Father, I know enough
of Your Word and will,
to realize that such ideas
are completely out of line.

Help me keep in mind
the defining comparison You made.
"Be subject," You said,
"as the church is subject to Christ,"
Who is both Head and Savior.
Love is the proper and automatic response
to love, wherein Another
gives Himself for us.
And such responding love
gives and serves and sacrifices,
even as the love that begot it.

Let it be so in my marriage, Lord.
Do not let me develop an attitude
wherein I sit and muse critically on

whether my husband is giving me
      the right amount and quality of love
   to which I can justifiably respond.
You are perfect, Lord,
   and Your love is perfect.
My husband is not,
   and there will always be defects
      detectable in His love for me.

Make me ready to forgive and overlook,
      even as I pray that he and You
         will forgive and overlook
      the failings in my response of love, too.

Make me ready to work with and for him,
      whether I feel he deserves it or not.

Divorce?

Lord Jesus, I have a deep conviction
      that divorce is wrong.
I feel that when two become one
      and make their sincere promises
they should keep their union
      holy and unbroken all through life.

I feel it is quite similar
      to the promise we've made You.

Knowing Your love for us,
    rejoicing in Your self-sacrifice,
I realize we owe You our unending love.

Yet there are those who tell me
    I'm out of date,
    I'm not being realistic.
They ask, "Which is better —
    a loveless marriage or a divorce?"

Lord, I know there are marriages
    that are horrible mistakes.
I'm aware that You know it too.
You have shown Your concern
    that no one should live
        a lifetime of marital hell.
It was You who said
    that a person is free to break off
from a spouse who defiles the marriage bed
    with other companions;
and that when someone does not respect
    the sacred responsibilities of marriage
and just walks out on the other,
    let him go.
The bond is already broken.

But, Lord Jesus, isn't it right
    that husbands and wives should try
        to keep their family together
        even if there may be sufficient reason
            to dissolve it?

You know, Lord, I don't mean
    just to try to hold an empty shell together
but to rebuild and remodel the marriage
    to make it good.

It's so easy to find things wrong —
    "We don't love each other anymore!"
    "We're just not compatible!"

But Lord, isn't that the time
    to pray and work together
        to correct what's wrong?
    to begin to grow together?
    to learn to help each other?
    to learn to forgive each other?

If things ever do go wrong
    (though I pray they never will),
give us enough deep feeling
    for marriage and for each other
that we do not even entertain the idea
    of running away.
Through our strugglings make us strong
    and capable builders of the kind of home
        You intended for us in the first place.

2
Live-a-Day Problems

Appearance

Dear Lord, it is often said,
    "You can tell a man by his clothes."
I know, and Your Word confirms it,
    that this is not always true.
Appearances can be deceiving.

But I also know,
    and Your Word confirms this too,
that appearance can tell a lot
    about a person's attitudes.

That's why I'm asking for Your help,
    that neither my attitudes
        nor my appearance
    become slipshod and careless
        now that I am comfortably married.

Just because I cornered the market
    and took my man out of circulation,
        is no excuse for me to let down.
The fact that my husband,
    at work or lunch or en route
        is continually rubbing elbows
    with relatively attractive young women
        who pay considerable attention
            to apparel, cosmetics, and poise

should be reason enough to get me
to remove the pink curlers
before he gets home,
and have the house and myself
in a semblance of order.

A semblance of order!
I pray, Lord, that as You look into my heart
You see more than that —
more than a "semblance"
of anything.
Help me ever more and more
to "be," not just "resemble" —
whether this apply to my role
as a wife, a mother,
or a Christian.
Build me up, through Your Word,
to be the real article.
That when You look into my heart,
You recognize true faith,
not a facsimile of faith,
and see that I am not just playing
at being a reborn child of God.

Let that same genuineness
be apparent in my home and family too.

Communication

Dear Father, I feel so much
    the need of talking things over with You.
Sometimes it gets so quiet around the house
    and lonely, too.

Not that there isn't noise. There is!
    Children at play,
    Telephone jangling,
    TV or radio droning —
but that's the trouble. It's mostly noise!

Not that there isn't anything to do.
    My husband may tease when he gets
    home —
        "What's the matter, dear? Have a
        bad day?
        Fall off your rocking chair?" —
    But he knows too and appreciates
        that there's a lot to making a home
            and keeping up a family.

Not that I don't have a lot of chance to talk.
    If I wanted to, I could spend all day
        sitting, gossiping, or playing cards.
    There's always plenty of opportunity for
    that.

But talking and talking things over
        just aren't the same.
There are thoughts to be expressed,
        concerns to be spelled out,
        ideas and problems to be discussed,
        dreams and plans to be shared —
yet there are few with whom I can
        or would care to
                talk over such things.

I can and must with my loved one.
        Help him to realize how important this is.

I can and must with You.
        Help me to realize how important this is.

Love communicates.
        This is a part of its very nature.
I need but think of You to be reminded of
this.
Your words and Christ the living Word
        bespeak Your love to me.
They leave me no doubt that You desire
        and have worked out my eternal good.

Lord, draw us so close to each other
        that we may really communicate —
                not just words but love —
        so that it can be seen and understood.
And draw us close to You,
        that You can be sure of our love, too.
                as we are of Yours.

Togetherness

Blessed Savior, once long ago,
    when You were with Your loved ones
        on the slope of a hill,
You promised,
    "Lo, I am with you always,
    even unto the end of the world."

We still take heart
    in Your promise today, Lord.
It matters not that we cannot
    see Your footprints in the dust,
    feel the touch of Your hand,
    or hear the sound of Your voice.
We know Your presence is real
    and sense Your power and love
        in our daily life.

Let me learn from this, Lord Jesus,
    the secret of togetherness.
Bless us with a similar togetherness
    in our home and family.

Give us one heart and one mind, Lord,
    so that even though our paths
    lead in various directions each day,
we may still always arrive together
    at the same goal.

Make us like the two hands of a clock —
    with one motivating power,
        one pivotal point,
            one purpose in act.

Grant us the ability
    to enjoy the hours we are together
    and to sense our togetherness
        in the hours we are apart.

Keep us both mindful
    that togetherness is more
        than just being together.
You can pour oil on water;
    They seep everywhere together.
But what do they have in common?
    What do they mean to each other?

We need more than a laminated marriage,
    a side-by-side existence.
We need to live in each other,
    for each other,
        through each other.
Help us to attain such togetherness, Jesus!

Pastime and Recreation

Father, help us to enjoy
　　the time we spend together.

How often we complain
　　that we have so little time
　　　　for family recreation.
This may be true, and it may call
　　for a determined attempt
　　to rearrange our days and hours.
But it may also be true
　　that we do not make good use
　　　　of the time we have together.

Father, help us to plan intelligently
　　how we can get the most good
　　　　out of our leisure time.
Don't let either of us
　　try to pressure the other
　　　　to conform to his or her fancy.

It wouldn't be right
　　for my husband to insist that
since he puts in a semimonotonous
　　eight hours a day,
　　　　five days a week,
I should have to tag at his heels
　　and put up with dusty campgrounds
so he can go fishing every week.

But then, it wouldn't be right either
     for me to keep pulling him out
to the type of excitement I like,
     when a little peace and quiet
may be what he really needs.

Father, give us enough sense
     to plan and do
what will be good for both of us.

May our love be great enough
     that, for the sake
          of doing things together,
we will swallow a few dislikes
     and inconveniences.
Don't let apparent reluctance
     or begrudged participation
          ruin it all.

Let love be our guide.
     For love will find the way
to make our moments of pastime
     truly enjoyable.

Slow Us Down, Lord!

Busy, busy, busy!
    Where does the time go, Lord?
Oh, I know where all right!
    I complain about it enough
        that I ought to know.

Cooking, cleaning, sewing,
    washing, ironing, shopping —
        monotonous routine;
telephone solicitors, door-to-door salesmen —
        irritating routine.

Lord, often I feel like a bowl of Jello,
    jiggling all over.
Then day is done, and what is changed?
It will be the same again tomorrow.
Busy! Busy! Busy!

Lord, show me that I may not be as busy
    as I sometimes like to think I am.
Help me see that often I am rushed
    and have that harried, hurried feeling
        because I used my time poorly.

How often I've berated the fact
    that I have so little time for prayer,
        so little time to talk to You,

yet I manage to squeeze in quite a bit
    just chatting with the neighbors.

I've regretted so often that,
    when we were having a heart-to-heart talk,
the telephone rang,
    and we never got back to the point.
Why do I feel that the intruder
    at the other end of the line
        is more important than my family,
    that I should always run to heed
        the tyrannical clamor?
It's forgivable, isn't it, Lord,
    that sometimes I just not answer the phone?

And, Lord, why am I so foolish that I feel
    every worthwhile club or group
has a right to make demands on my time
    or on my husband's time?

Slow us down, Lord,
    that we may take more time
        for each other
        and for You.

If hours be limited,
    teach us to use them wisely.
Teach us to put first things first.
    First things — our family — and You.

Money

Dear Lord, it has oft been said,
    "The best things in life are free."

We make no monthly payments
    on the air we breathe,
    on the warmth and light of the sun,
    on the beauty of surrounding nature;
they are ours to enjoy freely.

We pay no fees for Your forgiving love,
    for the hope of eternity
        offered us in Christ.
These too are ours —
    no charges, no strings attached.

Yet, Lord, I have also learned that
    when one provides for the necessities in life,
        he does not do so without price.
It doesn't take long after marriage
    before one discovers budgets
    and learns that there are limitations
        in the art of spending.

Lord, teach me the value of money!
Don't let me give my husband
    the feeling that he must shield me
        from the hard, cold facts
           of family finance.

If there need be concern
over the judicious use of our income,
let me share that concern with him.

Give me self-control.
Surely I am mature enough
to understand that I do not need
everything I would like,
and reasonable enough
not to use purchasing power
to try to impress others.

Let me also see money
as a means of carrying out
Your will as well as ours.
Let me taste the joy
that comes with unselfishness,
the thrill of contributing
to the well-being of others.

Keep me also constantly mindful
that all we have comes from You.
May our using reflect our gratitude
in receiving.

Trust and Jealousy

Dearest Savior, we all learn,
    usually the hard way,
that every action
    produces a reaction.
Yet how seldom we give forethought
    as to what might happen
because of what we do or say —
    or don't say.

Jealousies can smolder,
    even when there is no fuel
        for a fire.
Someone just strikes a match,
    and it won't stop smoking.

Lord, give us quiet confidence
    in each other
that we be protected from the sparks
    of incendiary suspicion,
that could so badly sear our home.

And Lord, give us enough sense
    to watch our words and acts
that we give no cause
    for distrust to be inflamed.

Without trust and confidence
    we could easily imagine the worst
        almost any time.

Work alone separates us
    over one third of every day.
And meetings and other activities —
    business, church, school,
        and who knows what else —
cut into even more
    of our little time together.
There's plenty of ground
    on which to build suspicion,
        if that's what we want to do.

But Lord, we don't!
Help us therefore to act
    that we give no occasion
        for jealousy
    and that we also react
        accordingly.

Lord Jesus, I think the finest pattern
    relates to You.
"We love You" —
    that's our proper reaction!
It's the only response befitting
    Your real and proper action —
"You first loved us!"

Lord, help us so to live,
    constantly acting and reacting
        in love and trust.

Forgive

Dearest Lord Jesus, it seems strange
    that I should have to ask for the power
      and the will to forgive.
But I must!

There's hardly a day that passes
    without my praying,
      "Forgive us . . . as we forgive those . . ."
What bothers me
    is that sometimes I don't forgive them —
      even him to whom I've pledged my love.

"Love begins at home," it's often said.
    Forgiveness must too.

I suppose, looking at it logically,
    that's where it can be quite difficult.
When you're very close to someone,
    and his major mistakes
      and minor failings
    are constantly in your line of vision,
there's always the temptation
    to make a loud, prolonged issue of it.
Prevent me from doing it, Lord!

Keep me conscious of the fact
    that he has the same point of vantage
      of me and my shortcomings.

Yet I count on his willingness
     to forgive and forget.

Let me see myself
     through Your eyes, blessed Savior.
For only as I see what You forgave in me
     and how You sacrificed Yourself in my be-
     half
only thus can I begin to grasp the dimensions,
     the breadth and depth,
          of true forgiving love.

Give me that kind of a love, Lord Jesus!
Let such be my love to all
     whose paths cross mine,
          and especially to those few
     whose whole lives are merged with mine.

So that, when aggravations arise,
     I do not need to ask,
          "How many times, Lord? Seven?"
     nor need to be told,
          "Seventy times seven."
May ours ever be the blessedness
     of forgiving and being forgiven.

Dreams and Plans

Lord, make us dreamers!

There's no difficulty
    in getting down to earth.
Our daily cares and labors
    exert sufficient gravitational force.
The trick lies in
    not forgetting how to fly.

Lord, while we live,
    with two feet firmly planted
        on the ground,
    enable our spirits to soar
        as we look ahead.

Fill us with plans and dreams
    and hopes and goals,
    not worries and anxieties
        as we face tomorrow, Lord.
We know better than that.

Let us see our horizon
    as more than a limitation.
Let us see it as a point we reach —
    a point from which we can see
        new promises
    and find thrilling joy in them.

Fill us with hopes and dreams, Lord!
Let them also express
    our confidence in You.
We dare to plan,
    for we know
we do not enter tomorrow alone.

I'm Tired!

Dear Father, You,
    who willed into being
        the heavens and the earth
            — and us,
    six days You worked.
Then on the seventh,
    after the wonders of creation
        had become tangibly real,
    You rested.

Many's the day, Father,
I feel like just lying there and resting
    before the work is done
        or even started.

I say I'm so tired, Father.
    Am I?

Or am I bored, depressed,
       just not very anxious
              to look another day in the face?
Why am I so ready
       to pull into my shell,
when I could be living
       such an excitingly creative life?

Sleep is a time of reconditioning,
       when You renew and prepare us —
              not for more sleep
       but for the awakeness
              and aliveness of a new day.

Lord, help me see clearly
       and accept enthusiastically
              the inviting opportunity
                     of each new day.
Keep me aware of how
       You have equipped me
              to make the most of it.

As the shining sun proclaims Your glory,
       and the singing birds Your praise,
              may I also be a living psalm each day.
I know all of us would benefit.

It's obvious how one person's sour attitude
       can cause an acid condition
              in the rest of the family.

It's obvious also how a cheery smile
        can snap others out of it
            when they feel tired and depressed.

So brighten me, Father!
        Make me alive to Your goodness and
            mindful of my cause for joy,
        that it erase the furrows from all our brows.

Temper! Temper!

O Lord, how often we fly into tantrums
        over some little "nothing"
that we feel in our own minds
        is really "something."

"Temper! Temper!" we have often scolded
        when children clenched their teeth
            or held their breath,
        because something didn't please them.
Yet how often we truly act
        as spunky and spoiled and foolish
            as any child.

It happens so spontaneously —
        stamping the foot, pointing the finger,
and screaming in indignation
        when something angers us.

Looking back on a few of those times,
    I realize that it accomplished very little,
        if anything.
It was only when we sat down
    and discussed things coolly and logically
        that any good came of it
    or any problem was corrected.

There are times when anger is necessary.
You became angry, too —
    when people were desecrating Your temple
    or
        when men were ready to point the finger
            at someone else's sin.
Oh, how angry You were!

Anger at the proper moment is very much in
place.
    But not "temper" —
        the satisfying of that momentary desire
            to really tell someone off.

Keep me from acting like a spoiled child
    in front of those I love.
It seems they always are the ones
    to bear the brunt of my flare-ups.
What we say in anger we so often regret
    for a long time to come.

O Lord, help me to keep my emotions under
control
    and to keep my tongue from lashing
        those I love.

Honesty

Dearest Savior, in a world
    where we are all tempted to use
        varying forms of dishonesty
    to avoid momentary unpleasantness,
it means so much to hear You say,
    "I am the Truth!"

How carefully did the prejudiced
    fine-tooth-comb You
in a fruitless attempt to prove
    it was not really so.

But You are!
You are who You claimed to be.
You did what You said You would.
And what You've promised
    I know confidently will be so.

Lord, make me like that —
    honest, trustworthy.
Not brutally honest, Lord!
There's no reason to cut and hurt
    my loved ones with a sharp tongue.

Lord Jesus, You chided and corrected,
    but Your love always showed through.
You always helped and
    never belittled.

Even when You point up our sin,
    it is to apply healing forgiveness.
Let me also thus speak "truth in love."

Sometimes, Lord, I feel like
    saying absolutely nothing.
Things irritate or seem wrong,
    and I bite my tongue as if
        nothing had happened.
But isn't that dishonest too?
Give me always the courage to speak,
    to confess my true feelings,
and the readiness
    to let others do the same.

Give us such confidence in one another
that we truly dare to open our hearts;
that we do not feel the need
    of projecting a polished image,
and that we can just be ourselves
    and love each other for it.

The Gift of Understanding

Dearest Lord Jesus, can a person
    truly understand anyone
        other than oneself?

Sometimes I wonder
    if I truly understand
        my husband or my children.
Their ways become my way,
    and their problems become mine,
only when I deliberately assume them.
And even then — little beyond the degree
    to which they open up their hearts.
But we need so very much
    to really understand one another.

Hope and faith are mine, Lord Jesus,
    because of Your understanding love.
I look to You as the One
    who really knows and cares.
For You came
    to fill our shoes,
    to tread our paths,
    to face our trials,
    to shoulder our burdens,
    to counter our wrongs;
and even more —
    to assume our guilt,
    to bear our punishment,
    to free us eternally,
though it cost life to gain life.
None of this would ever have been
    if You didn't understand, Lord!

Give me an understanding heart, Jesus,
    especially for those with whom
        my life is closely joined.

Let me learn how
    to see what they see,
    to feel how they feel,
    to sense their hurts,
    to thrill to their joys.

Don't let us be blocks in a box
    but living, potent elements
constantly working in, with,
    and through each other —
not just touching
    but truly affecting one another
        for our total good.

On Getting Ahead

Dearest Lord Jesus, day after day
    I see my husband head for work,
        and often I know,
            by his expressionless face,
    that that's the last place he cares to be.
And many's the night that he comes home,
    scars of frustration clearly visible.

I know, dear Savior, that, to some extent,
    he's doing it for me —
        to provide a comfortable home
        and a measure of security
            for the days to come.

I wish I could relieve him of his daily
pressures.
I cannot bear his burden,
    but I can keep it from becoming unbear-
    able.

Teach me, Lord, to do my part in helping him
    by sharing joyfully and enthusiastically
        with him the things we have
    rather than dolefully deploring
        the things we do not have.
Help me to live contentedly within our income,
    so that my spending and his earning
        are not competing with each other,
    making him feel he must constantly drive
    himself.
Show us both that we do not need a lot
    to find true happiness —
        as long as we have each other
        and as long as we have You.

Though You were rich, Lord Jesus,
    yet for our sakes You became poor
        that we, through You, might be rich.
Now show us, Lord, how rich we really are.
    The highest position
        is reigning with You forever.
    The peak of wealth
        is the crown of eternal glory.
    The greatest "in"
        is to be acclaimed Your very own.
All this we already have through You.

We also have each other.
Now give us also the peace of contentment
    that it may truly underlie our daily life
and help us determine our goals and paths.

Thin Skins

Dearest Lord, there are enough wounds
    and bruises in life
without our imagining more
    or making them more
        than they really are.

When two live closely as one,
    there will be times
        when we hurt each other.
But wounds quickly heal,
    unless self-pity
        causes them to fester.
Don't let either of us
    waste our time
nursing our bruises —
    especially when so many of them
        are imaginary!

Lord Jesus, Your hurt was real,
    deliberately inflicted.

Yet You saw fit to pray:
    "Father, forgive them;
        they know not what they do."
And even more —
    You saw fit to give Yourself
        for their forgiveness.

And I?

Keep me from taking offense
    when no offense is intended.
Keep me from finding slur and insult
    in unfortunate though innocent talk.
Soothe my raw and sensitive nerves
    with the balm of love.

And, dear Lord,
    when the hurt is real,
        perhaps even intended,
give me the power to forgive.

Language

"May the words of my mouth . . .
    be acceptable in Thy sight,
O Lord, my Strength
    and my Redeemer."

The ability to speak
    is one of Your finest gifts.
I'm so grateful, Lord,
    that I do not live in
the world of silence,
    known only to the deaf.

But sometimes silence
    has its points, too.
Show me when to keep quiet
    as well as when
        and what to speak.

Help me to develop the habit
    of thinking before I speak.
One verbal blowout can cause
    a whole family to veer off course
        and bring lasting hurt.

Let love dictate my speech.

Love for You —
    wherein my lips are sealed
        to profane or blasphemous talk,
            intended or unintended.
Love for my husband —
    wherein I will always attempt
        to encourage and build him up
    rather than nag or belittle.
Love for my children —
    wherein I will train and guide —
        not just scold and restrict.

Love for all others —
wherein I will avoid gossip
and everything else that is
none of my business.

Keep me mindful too, O Lord,
that the unguarded word
does as much harm
as one willfully spoken
and that it is a revealing gauge
of my true character.

Use my tongue as a tool,
well-designed to serve
Your purposes —
not as a dangerous weapon, Lord!

Daily Tasks

They say, "The hand that rocks the cradle
rules the world."
Lord, sometimes I feel
like giving it a good shaking!

Often I feel imprisoned —
caught in a domestic trap.
Cribs and toys,
sinks and ovens,

vacuums and washers
    surround me like sentries,
making sure I do not escape.

On my limited excursions
    into the outside world,
I see other women
    obviously enjoying a freedom
        I seldom taste.

Back in the confines
    I plot my escape.
I visualize myself
    caught up in the whirl.
Let someone else do
    the little, unimportant things.
I'm going to find excitement
    and be noticed.

O Lord, wake me up!
    What is life all about anyway?

Does idle lolling in plush salons,
    being looked on as
        "someone who is someone"
    mean anything much at all?

Let me see how green the grass is
    on my side of the fence.
Help me to see —
    not the frying pan

but the loving and admiring glance
of a very proud husband;
not the washer and dryer
but a well-groomed family,
whose whole appearance
shouts out my love for them.

Callus and cross
predominated in Jesus' life.
But it is obvious enough
that Jesus looked beyond them.
He saw the lonely and the crowds
who needed His love.
In His love for them
He assumed the daily grind
and the bitter end.
And I in Christ am eternally blessed.

Lord, help me appreciate
the worth of my daily task.
Let love override
the drudgery of it all.
Whatever my hand finds to do,
let me do it with all my might —
for them
and for You.

Work Obligations

Father, I have to talk to You.
When I try to talk to my husband
    about what's on my mind,
he usually shakes his head and says,
    "Honey, you just don't understand!"

It's about his work, Father.
I know how important it is.
I know what heavy responsibilities he bears.
I know the demands and pressures he faces.
I know the constant competition is unnerving.

I hate to see him the victim of unjust demands.
I hate to see anyone walk all over him.
I hate to see him become estranged
    from the rest of the family,
        because he has so little time at home,
        because he is so tense when he is at home.

Father, I don't mean to criticize.
    It's only because I love him so very much
        that I speak up at all.
But so often it backfires.
    He feels he has to leap to his defense,
        and I don't want that.
He has enough fighting to do each day.

But I know that when pressures become too great
    and the pace too fast,
bodies break down;
    minds, too!
Father, I want to safeguard against such a day.
Enable us to talk about these things now
    and understand each other's concerns.

Let me help him keep the proper perspective;
    he's more important than his job;
    so is our family.
I don't want the honor of his position
    or a big income.
I just want him, Father —
    alive and healthy and happy.

Help me show him I want
    only what is best —
not just for the family
    but for him too.

The Business Trip

"The Lord watch between thee and me
    while we are absent one from another."
How often we've had occasion
    to speak these priceless words;
    how seldom we do.

Yet, heavenly Father,
        isn't that what we need
                more than anything else —
        that You watch over us both
                in our hours apart?

Oh, how I dislike
        our days of separation.
Maybe I'm feeling sorry for myself.
But I'm sure he doesn't like it
        any more than I do.

I remind myself that there are wives
        who have it so much worse.
When some kiss their husbands goodbye,
        they know they will not see them
                for many, many months —
        months fraught with constant danger.

But Lord, the fact that others
        have similar problems, even worse,
                doesn't eliminate mine.
There are those who say,
        "You have to get used to it.
        You just have to develop
                a life of your own."
But I don't want to develop
        a life of my own.
It doesn't have to be that way,
        does it, Father?

We can still be completely one,
　　even when we are apart.
The fact that You are with us both,
　　watching over us both,
　　　　brings me so much peace.

Watch over him, heavenly Father,
　　especially in his hours alone.
I trust him implicitly,
　　but I realize that
Satan had the audacity
　　to tempt even Jesus.
Keep him sound in every way
　　and speed his safe return.

And watch over me, Father.
　　Fill my days of aloneness
　　　　with a feeling of Your closeness.
Use our being apart
　　to make us appreciate
　　　　how wonderful it will be
　　when we are together again.

I'm Bored!

Father, sometimes I think
　　I watch too many dramas
　　　　on television.

They weave such an inviting web,
    as they glamorize forbidden fruit.
The illicit and secret romance
    seems a welcome change
        from household routine.
Usually the intruding Casanova
    comes out shinier than the husband.
And though the cause
    of the virtuous wife be lauded,
they play up that last lusty look
    at the still-appealing siren.
When there's no third party in the plot,
    they make it seem as if a good marriage
        is only fun and games, excitement, and
        new adventure every day.

Sometimes then, by comparison,
    the real thing looks slightly drab.
But it's not!
    Unless we let it get that way.
When the bulk of one's time
    is spent in the house,
one is bound to get pretty bored.
Keep me mindful
    of what it's really all about.
I'm not just keeping house;
    I'm making a home.
I'm making our home
    the most significant place —
        at least to us —
    in the whole wide world.

With Your guidance and blessing, Father,
    I can help create a haven
        of peace and love.
Maybe I should say "a heaven,"
    for You are also a part of it.

I'm not darning socks
    and wiping noses
    and burning biscuits
    and pushing shopping carts;
I'm helping to shape lives,
    the lives of those
        nearest and dearest to me.

Boring?
Father, help me to see better.

Selfishness

How long does it take, Lord,
    to learn to think in terms
        of "we" and "us" and "ours"?

How awkward
    those early days of marriage,
when our individual possessions
    suddenly became joint property!

It still seems that everything
    should be divided into two piles
and be clearly and properly labeled
    "his" and "hers."
There's almost a feeling of resentment
    when one or the other ignores
        the invisible boundary.

When does one grow out of this?
It's possible — isn't it, Lord? —
    that a person could go
        through all of life,
never wanting to relinquish
    a personal claim,
never really wanting
    to share at all.

I'm impressed, Lord,
    that when You brought
        this wonderful world into being,
You didn't hoard it
    for Your personal pleasure.
You told the happy couple,
    as You invited them to use it,
        to enjoy it and
    to benefit from
        Your master production.

When Christ gained the "crown of life,"
    He shared it with us.

Lord, give us such unselfishness —
    towards each other,
    towards others,
    towards You.
Let such be the dimensions
    of our love.

One in Faith

Dearest Lord, I think
    that some of the most beautiful words
ever uttered by the lips of woman
    were the words of Ruth:
"Whither thou goest, I will go;
    and where thou lodgest, I will lodge.
Thy people shall be my people,
    and thy God my God."

As far as I'm concerned,
    they still are the last word
        on real togetherness.
True oneness is more than just
    going together,
        or living together —
more than suddenly merging two clans
    into one big bunch of in-laws
and trying to get along with them all.

Isn't the ultimate in oneness
    the sharing of faith?
Sharing the inner hopes and joys
    that are ours in Christ?
They say that Bahamian fishermen
punch a small hole in the shells
    of the beautiful queen conches
        they find.
Then they tie them together
    and just drop them on the beach.
They know they will still be there
    when they return for them.
For though the animals are very much alive
    and will move towards freedom,
they will all pull
    in opposing directions
and get nowhere —
    other than the chowder pot.

So many families succumb
    to that danger.
They pull in so many directions at once;
    they all end up losers.

Lord, make us a family
    that enjoys complete togetherness.
May the love of Jesus be a part
    of that togetherness.

Make us a family that
    prays together,

worships together,
grows together in the Word, and
is alive to Christ.

In such deep oneness
may we find Your blessing.

Breadwinning

When one has food to eat each day,
prayers of thanks can easily become
a thoughtless routine,
even though we acknowledge You, Father,
as the One "from whom all blessings
flow."

When one enjoys a husband
who brings home a paycheck every payday,
she can take this for granted too.
Father, let me never lose my gratitude
at having a husband
who cares enough for me and ours
to work so hard on our behalf.

Help me to carry out my end of the line —
those tasks and responsibilities
that are the unique contribution
a wife can make to the well-being
and happiness of the family.

Sometimes, heavenly Father,
    I toy with the idea of getting out and away
        and bringing in another income.
That little extra something
    can sound pretty good —
        the change of pace too.

I know there are times when outside
employment
    may be advisable, even necessary.
But don't let me be fooled into thinking
    that greater financial independence
        or a private career
    are more to be desired
        than the satisfaction
    of being a good wife and mother.

Isn't dependence on each other
    — not independence —
basic to the idea of being "one"?
All too often two jobs
    have come to mean two separate ways
        and eventually two separate lives.
I've noticed the same in this —
    the more I've let outside interests
        take me away from You, Father,
    the cooler my love,
        the shallower my faith.
And then, when I needed You most,
    I sought You least.

Let nothing disturb or destroy
    my closeness with my husband
    or my closeness with You.

A Sense of Humor

Lord, let the joy I've found in You
    pervade the atmosphere in our home.
Help me to be a truly happy person.
Bring my family happiness through me.

It's disheartening to see how people
    in potentially strong families
        will snap and snarl,
        bicker and bite,
        and really make life miserable
            for one another.
And it's not that
    they don't love each other.

They seem to have the problem
    of thick heads and thin skins,
and that's a pretty bad combination.
They have lost one of Your choicest gifts —
    a sense of humor.
What a tragic loss!

I recall that verse in Proverbs:
    "A cheerful heart has a continual feast."

A person does not need a lot
    to have a full life.
A happy and grateful heart
    enables even the poor
        to enjoy what he has,
      while others, who have much more,
        can be miserably malcontent.

We can get along
    without a lot in life.
But don't let us lose our happy spirit.

Sometimes we tend to take our problems,
    or even ourselves
        much too seriously.
We need to take You
    much more seriously, Lord.
But we would do well
    to laugh at ourselves a little more.
Even correction and criticism
    are accepted much more graciously
when they are administered
    with love and a humorous quip.

So, Lord, I do not feel the need
    of asking for very much.
But I do ask for this —
    a cheerful heart
    and sense of humor
        for us all.

Sharing Responsibility

Dearest Savior, I do so appreciate
    our life together.
        My husband means so much to me!

But when routines become established,
    it is so easy
        to take so much for granted.
Each day without fail
    my husband puts in long hours at work
and without fail
    brings home a regular paycheck.
I seldom give it
    a second thought.
And each day I whittle away
    at my daily chores
        till he returns.

It's good, Lord,
    that we each have our job to do.
When you work at something together
    it takes on double meaning.
I know that's why our home
    means so much to us.
Ours may be differing responsibilities,
    but we are both doing our part
        towards our family good.

I know it could easily deteriorate
into a less desirable situation.

Were it not for love,
there could always be
a way to make
his burden heavier,
and mine lighter.
The opportunity is always there.

I suppose, if I wanted to,
I could fritter away the day
on neighborhood coffee hours,
and then complain,
when he comes home,
"A woman's work is never done."

But, dear Savior, I know
that our responsibilities are part
of our togetherness.
I wouldn't want it to be
any other way.
That's how we help each other
and live for each other.

You understand that
better than I do, Lord!
You came not to do Your part,
but to bear our whole burden
for our eternal good.

Make me more like You, Savior.
    Make us both like that.
If both of us
    not only do our part
but even try
    to lighten the other's load,
what a wonderful home we can have!

Social Status

A lot of time has passed, Lord Jesus,
    since You gently reproved the mother
who came requesting preeminence
    for her two sons.
What could delight a mother's heart more
    than to see her boys
in positions of greatest glory
    in the kingdom of heaven?
Oh, how other mothers
    might envy her eternally!
We still make the same mistakes.
    Will we never learn, Jesus?

Why do we so often
    ruin our health and lives,
sometimes even sacrifice our souls,
    for something of questionable worth?

I say "we," but I know
　　that frequently it's the wife
who ruins her husband's health,
　　because she wants to be
　　　　"somebody."

Lord, is not life more than —
　　what you have?
　　where you live?
　　what others think of you?
　　position or status?

What is important?
　　Knowing the "best" people?
　　Membership in the country club?
　　Two new cars?
　　Belonging to the right groups?
　　Wearing originals, one-of-a-kinds?
　　Weekly appointments
　　　　at an exclusive hairdresser's?
　　Pictures on the society page?

Lord, I know there's nothing wrong
　　with most of those things.
　　It's the attitude!
　　That's where the danger lies.
When suddenly such things seem
　　the most important of all
and they become the big goal,
　　that's when we'd better be on guard.

Don't ever let me forget, Lord,
    that I already do have real status.
Talk about status!
Almighty God has openly acclaimed me
    as His very own child.
My Brother is
    the King of kings and Lord of lords.
My Brother thought enough of me
    to give up His life for me.
When this whole world is in ashes,
    I shall still live
        in the best home of all
    with my eternal family.
I don't have to fight to be somebody!
By Your grace I already am!

Impatience

Dearest Jesus, when You look at me,
    I fear I remind You more of Martha
        than of Mary.

I don't mean that I
    would rather wait on tables
        than listen to Your Word.
I don't think that is even
    a fair appraisal of Martha.

82

What I do mean is that I,
    like Martha,
am often inclined to want
    to foist my priorities
        on other people
and to become quite impatient,
    even indignant,
        when they do not conform.

It happens even at home;
I get impatient with my husband
    and impatient with my children.
But why, Lord?
It is generally only a matter
    of one person's will
        taking precedence
            over the other's,
when neither was right or wrong
    from the very beginning.
Oh, yes, there are times
    when it is warranted.
Sometimes even your loved ones
    let you down.
That's why I need You to bless me
    with the gift of patient love
        like Yours, blessed Savior!

Prophets and preachers
    could size up the masses,
    proclaim stern judgment,
    and wait for it to happen.

Yet You, in striking contrast,
    offered more promise,
        more love, more hope,
and guaranteed it
    with Your lifeblood.
Our life has meaning,
    and we have a future,
because You have been
    patient with us, O Savior!

Lord, fill me
    with such patience
that the lives of those
    with whom I live and love
may be blessed by it too.

Taking Each Other for Granted

So often, as the years pass, Lord,
    the feeling comes crowding in,
"No one around here
    really appreciates me."

It is seldom true.
But it is true that we are slow
    in expressing our appreciation.

Why should it be so, Lord?
There is no place
    in this whole wide world
where love prevails
    so much as in the home;
No other place where people do
    so much for each other.
But how often do we stop
    to say "Thank you"?

How often do I thank my husband
    for being a hard worker,
        a good father and provider?
How often does he thank me
    for maintaining an atmosphere
        of warmth and brightness,
    of peace and love at home?
Lord, don't let us take anything for granted!
Wake us up to the magic
    of warm appreciation.

Towards You too, dear Lord!
We should sing Your praises
    every moment of every day.
We're surrounded by Your love.
Life, health, strength,
    home, food, clothing,
family, friends,
    guidance and protection,
forgiveness and eternal hope,
    an unending life in Christ —
all this is of Your love, freely given.

And our thanks?
    Like David we need to say:
"Bless the Lord, O my soul,
    and forget not all His benefits."
Lord, help us to pay properly
    the debt of appreciation we owe —
        to whom we owe it.

False Pride

Lord Jesus, I remember Your story
    of the guests at the banquet
who elbowed their way
    right up to the head table
only to meet the indignity
    of being asked to give up their seats
        to more deserving people.

How much better if they had come
    without airs —
to enjoy the gracious hospitality
    offered them,
not to use the joyous affair
    for self-aggrandizement.
"Pride goes before the fall."

When I enjoy the delicious feeling
    of being somewhat superior,

86

having truly succeeded
    where others have failed —
is not that also such pride?

When "I thank Thee
    that I am not as others,"
that I have the reputation
    of being an upright person —
is not that what You're warning about?
I know so many homes are harmed
    by the proud spirit.
If a husband or wife
    entertains such airs,
        it soon rubs off on the other,
    creating a reaction
        of inferiority and resentment.

Dear Jesus, fill me
    with Your spirit.
Let me not belittle
    in false humility
what You have made me
    or given me.
Let me receive all Your good gifts
    with thanksgiving
and see them all to be
    as wonderful as they are.

But let the glory go to You,
    the Giver —
        not to me!

Indecision

Dearest Lord Jesus,
 life is an unending succession
  of decisions, isn't it?

Some are big.
My marriage is the result
 of a careful decision.
Even my Christian faith and life
 are the result of decision,
based on the Spirit-filled conviction
 that You are our eternal Redeemer.

Some are little,
 involving not much more than
the selection of food
 for our daily meals,
or the choosing of a wardrobe
 that shows good taste.

Some decisions call for
 immediate action.
Give me the ability
 to respond wisely
  and quickly at such times.
Some decisions call for
 methodical study
  and long-range planning.

Give us the ability
    to work such things out together,
that the two of us may really be as one.

And, Lord Jesus, when decisions
    have been made,
make us mature and strong enough
    to stick with them.

There are bound to be honest mistakes.
    Don't let them turn us
        against each other
    with a sarcastic
        "I told you so!"

Don't let us go through life
    speculating about
        how it might have been,
    had we made the other choice.

Show us that it's better
    to have made a wrong decision
        and learned by it
than to make no decision at all.
And guide us
    that our decisions may be
    increasingly right
    in Your sight.

Disagreements

"A soft answer turns away wrath,
but a harsh word stirs up anger."
That's good advice for any time, Lord,
    but especially for those
        not-too-frequent,
    yet much-too-frequent,
        moments of disagreement.

It seems so unnecessary
    and unfortunate
that the peace and harmony,
    so prevalent in our home,
should ever be marred
    by quarrel or argument.

It really is unnecessary,
    isn't it, Lord?
I don't mean differences of opinion;
    they are bound to arise.
Nor do I mean discussing these differences;
    that has its definite value.

What I regret is
    our occasional inability
to prevent our discussions
    from degenerating into contention.

It soon enough becomes apparent
    that one really does not argue
        to establish what's right,
    but to save face.

The soft answer
    still is the way to win.
The sharp retort
    only prolongs the fight.
Keep us both conscious of this.
And give us enough true love
    and respect for each other
that we may ever be more interested
    in working closely together
than in tabulating individual victories.

"Come now, let us reason together."
It almost seems strange, Lord,
    that You, our almighty God,
should invite us to sit down
    and talk things over with You.
We would expect You just to tell us —
    and let it go at that.
You'd have every right to,
    especially when it concerns our sins.
Yet, instead of forcing us
    to grovel ashamedly at Your feet,
You spoke quietly of cleansing,
    of Your forgiveness,
        and offered further blessing.
You could have won the point
    and set us down properly;

and You did also issue
    stern words of warning.
But Your basic aim was love —
    Your love for us.

Father, make Your ways our ways!

Quiet Time

Oh Father, how I cherish
    our quiet times.

There's so much going on
    all day, every day.
It seems I keep flitting
    from one thing to the next
and accomplishing very little.

Even when I'm not caught up
    in a whirlwind of activity,
there's always something
    that disturbs or distracts,
so that quiet times
    come infrequently,
usually late at night,
    when the younger side of the family
        is tucked snugly in bed.

Even then, Father,
　　we sometimes lose it completely.
Our minds keep suggesting
　　that we may be missing something
　　　　by not having our TV set on.
Why, Father —
　　why is the quiet time
　　　　usually the last resort?
Why do we feel we must explore
　　every other possibility first?

We always enjoy
　　such moments together.
We find them most productive
　　in sharing our thoughts,
in feeling very close to each other.

In such moments we go
　　far beyond the superficial.
Dreams are revealed,
　and plans take shape —
the very materials that are needed
　　for making a life,
that lift us above the level
　　of just living an existence.

Father, You also are so much more
　　a part of our quiet times
　　　　than of our daily bustle.
I suppose it should be so.

I always remember how Jesus suggested
    that, when we pray,
we should "enter into the closet,"
    go into a place quiet and alone,
where we can talk to You
    without distraction of any kind.

It really works best that way.
    That's the whole point
        behind our quiet times.
Prayer and meditation
    come quite naturally,
though they be hurried and strained
    at other times.
We can speak out our faith,
    discuss our doubts
        and disagreements,
and pray about them,
    when we are alone together,
without looking at the clock.

Father, help us seek out
    times like this.
They are moments
    of special blessing and
    of special closeness.

Synthetic Escape

When one hears the music long enough,
    one begins to march to the beat.

I suppose it's to be expected, Lord,
    that I should begin to accept
    unquestioningly
        the idea that, come what may,
    "relief is just a moment away."
The electronic cyclops in our living room
    that has become the master of us all
        has put the point across pretty well.

No need to worry anymore!
    The world has managed successfully
        to produce a pill for everything!
Can't sleep? Mind awhirl?
    Take a pill, and sleep like a baby!
Tend to doze? Want to keep going?
    Take a pill, and get keyed up!
There are pills to stimulate
    and pills to sedate,
pills to induce motherhood
    and pills to counter conception.

Lord, I don't mean to sound cynical.
But I am concerned when I find myself
    running to the medicine cabinet
        before I run to You.

And I am concerned that,
    when things weigh heavily on my mind,
I tend to reach out for synthetic escape
    instead of You.

"God is our Refuge and Strength,
    a very present Help in trouble."
Lord, let me not just sing:
    "What a Friend we have in Jesus. . . .
        Take it to the Lord in prayer!"
Teach me to *do* just that!
For in You there is an answer to my
problems,
    not just temporary escape.
In You there is cure, not just relief.
Jesus came not to cover up our sin,
    but to "cleanse us from all sin."

It doesn't say,
    "With His stripes we are helped."
It assures,
    "With His stripes we are healed."

Lord, for my sake, for my family's sake,
when things go wrong,
    let me seek and find refuge
        and strength in You.

The Bridled Tongue

Dearest Lord, keep me busy!
    Not needlessly, but purposefully!

I want to be friendly with my neighbors,
    but I don't want to slip into the rut
        of daily coffee hours.
So often they degenerate into hunting trips;
    and it's usually
        open season on husbands,
    with an occasional potshot
        at anything that moves
            into the line of vision.

"The tongue is a fire," You've warned.
    "How great a forest is set ablaze
        by a small fire."
Rather than having me ignite
    or fan a destructive fire
        and leave a blackened image,
    keep me away from where the sparks
        are prone to fly.

When there are idle moments in a day
    and I can relax
        in the atmosphere of pleasant company,
    help me — and them —
        to use our tongues properly
            and responsibly.

"Speak the truth in love," You said.
You did!
Even when You exposed our sin,
You did it in love
    to lead us to Your forgiveness.

In every promise of eternal life,
    in Your every encouragement
to live consistently in Christ,
    I see truth in love.

It's just Your way, Lord!
    Of course, I know You're perfect.
I'm not!
    But I desire to be
        more perfect than I am.
Let it begin with my tongue —
    with the way I talk about others,
        about those I love.

Friends

Lord Jesus, I really feel bad
    that You've never been repaid
        with a friendship
    to match Yours to us.
You loved us all enough to die for us.

Usually our love is so shallow that
    we don't even live for You.
I wish You could taste a pure love
    as we enjoy Yours.

I am also grateful, Lord,
    that, through these years,
You have guided others my way
    so that their lives touched mine
and our hearts gradually became entwined
    in bonds of true friendship.
There is a tendency
    in this mobile, transient world of ours
        to give it up as a lost cause.
"What's the use," we end up saying.
        "You just about find a good friend,
            and then you lose her."
So we settle back and say,
        "Never again! It hurts too much!"

Lord, let my love reach out again,
    no matter how often it may have to be.
And let me not settle for second best
    by trying to satisfy my need
        in casual acquaintances.

I need someone special, someone who —
    in my moments of distress
        will lend a strengthening hand;
    in my moments of success
        will show true happiness;

in my moments of failure
    will uphold my worth;
in my moments of slate-cleaning
    will prove worthy of my confidence.

I have found all this
    in You, Lord Jesus.
Help me find it also in others,
    at least to a degree.
I pray that I may always have
    at least one such friend
        along each step of life's way
    and be such a friend in turn.

In Time of Sickness

Dearest Jesus, I find
    great strength and comfort
when I see how sensitive You were
    to the pains and tears
        of all around You.

You heard the quavering
    "Lord, have mercy!"
above the tumult of the crowd.

You felt the hope-filled hand
    that reached to touch Your robe,
despite the jostling of the crowd.

You heard!
You felt!
You heeded!
You healed!

So I cry for mercy.
So I reach for healing love.
Mine is naught but trust,
    for I know You, Lord!
I know Your will!
I know Your ways!

Buying a Home

Dearest Father, thank You
    for making possible this joyous day.

I doubt if Adam and Eve
    could have been more delighted
        over the Garden of Eden
than we are in owning
    and moving into our beautiful home.

I'm not comparing places, Lord.
    It's just that so many
        of the basic features are the same.
Not really the way it's built
    or how it looks.

It's our own little corner
of paradise.
We are together in it,
and You with us.

Now mine is the exciting joy
of furnishing it and
of softening and brightening it
with many loving touches.

It matters, doesn't it, Lord,
what one puts into a home?
One can so easily fill it
with so much worthless clutter.
That happens when one sees a home
in terms of things
instead of the people you love.

Lord, help me make this a real home —
not a museum
or storage shed.
Let me see and plan everything
in terms of love and life.
The home is to serve the family,
not vice-versa.
Give me enough common sense
to keep it that way.

May our home be filled with brightness
that radiates from inside us.

May happiness and beauty abound,
    strength and security be apparent,
peace and comfort predominate.

Lord, live in this our home
    as in our hearts.
Not as a guest, Lord,
    but as One who very much belongs.

Just One Last Word

Just one last word, Lord —
    and I can confine it to one word —
        "Thanks!"

    Thank You for life —
        his life,
        my life,
        our life in Christ.
    Thank You for love —
        Your love,
        his love.
    Thank You for marriage —
        companionship,
        oneness in purpose,
        togetherness in result.

Bless our marriage —
    today, and
    through all the years to come.
Bless us with Your presence.
Bless us with peace,
    hope,
    joy,
    tenderness —
in short, with all those blessings
    that You willed to be a part of marriage
        since the very beginning.